# HOLIDAY ORIGAMI

## Fumiaki Shingu

Mud Puddle Books
NEW YORK

Holiday Origami
Created by Fumiaki Shingu

© 2006 by Mud Puddle Books, Inc.

Mud Puddle Books, Inc.
54 W. 21st Street
Suite 601
New York, NY 10010
info@mudpuddlebooks.com

ISBN: 1-59412-169-9

Printed and bound in China

# CONTENTS

| | | |
|---|---|---|
| Introduction | | **4** |
| Explanation of Diagrams | | **5** |
| Folding Techniques | | **7** |
| Christmas | | **9** |
| | Star ★ | 10 |
| | Candle ★★ | 11 |
| | Christmas Tree ★★ | 14 |
| | Santa ★★★ | 16 |
| | Snowman ★★ | 19 |
| | Bell ★★★ | 22 |
| Hanukkah | | **25** |
| | Dreidel ★★ | 26 |
| Valentine's Day | | **28** |
| | Thumping Heart ★★ | 29 |
| | Present ★★★ | 32 |
| | Box | 32 |
| | Heart Decoration | 35 |
| | Candy ★★★ | 38 |
| Easter | | **40** |
| | Easter Bunny ★ | 42 |
| | Flower ★★ | 43 |
| | Leaves | 43 |
| | Blossom | 45 |
| Halloween | | **49** |
| | Bat ★★★ | 50 |
| | Ghost ★★ | 52 |
| | Jack O Lantern ★★★ | 55 |
| | Witch & Broom ★★★ | 59 |
| | Broom | 59 |
| | Witch | 61 |

★ Very Easy    ★★ Easy    ★★★ More Difficult

# INTRODUCTION

## THE MAGICAL WORLD OF ORIGAMI

**P**ICTURE A SQUARE PIECE OF PAPER.

Imagine that square piece of paper turning into an animal, a flower, a box or something that moves.

This is the timeless appeal of origami, the Japanese art of paper folding. Origami has been captivating people and holding them spellbound for more than a thousand years. It's believed that by folding, decorating and playing with paper you cultivate your creativity and spark your imagination.

It's easy to master the techniques of origami and, by practicing as much as you can, you develop your skills and quickly move on to more advanced steps and projects.

This book can be used by beginners and experts alike. The projects are classified according to their level of difficulty. Children and adults will readily find projects that match their skills.

It makes me very happy to share my origami experiences with you and I would be so pleased if my origami techniques provide you with joy and delight.

—Fumiaki Shingu
Tokyo 2006

# EXPLANATION OF DIAGRAMS

**Fold on the dotted line.**

**Fold backward on the dotted line.**

**Fold to make a crease and fold back.**

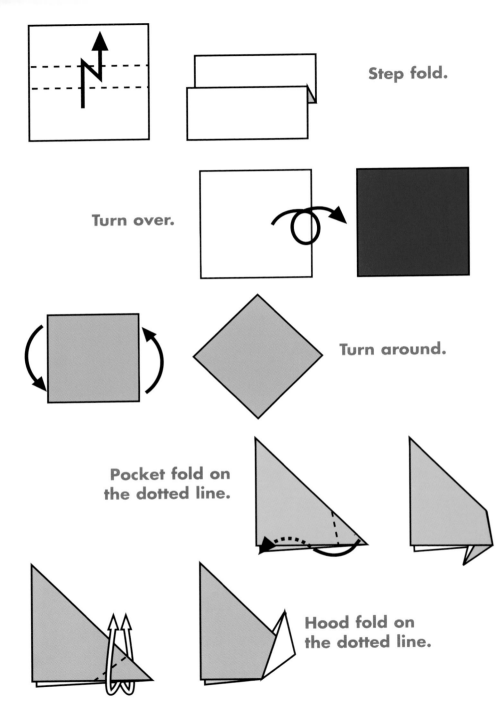

**Step fold.**

**Turn over.**

**Turn around.**

**Pocket fold on the dotted line.**

**Hood fold on the dotted line.**

# FOLDING TECHNIQUES

Take time to practice and master the three basic folds described here. They are used throughout this book and will allow you to create the beautiful projects that follow.

## Step Fold

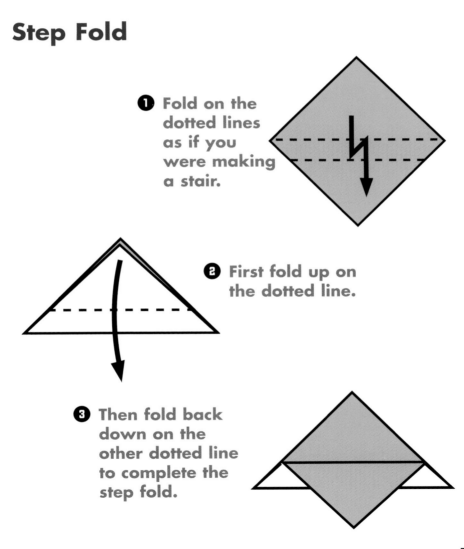

❶ Fold on the dotted lines as if you were making a stair.

❷ First fold up on the dotted line.

❸ Then fold back down on the other dotted line to complete the step fold.

# Pocket Fold

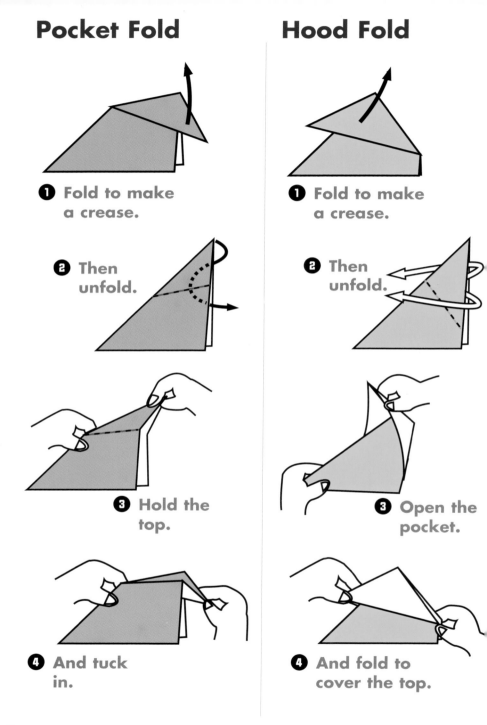

**1** Fold to make a crease.

**2** Then unfold.

**3** Hold the top.

**4** And tuck in.

# Hood Fold

**1** Fold to make a crease.

**2** Then unfold.

**3** Open the pocket.

**4** And fold to cover the top.

# STAR ★

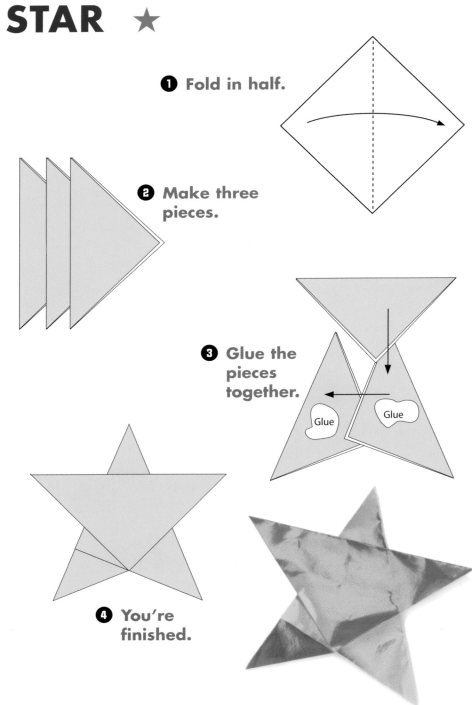

**1** Fold in half.

**2** Make three pieces.

**3** Glue the pieces together.

Glue

Glue

**4** You're finished.

# CANDLE ★★

① Fold on the dotted lines to make creases and unfold.

② Fold on the dotted lines to meet the center.

③ Fold on the dotted lines to meet the center.

④ Fold backward on the dotted line.

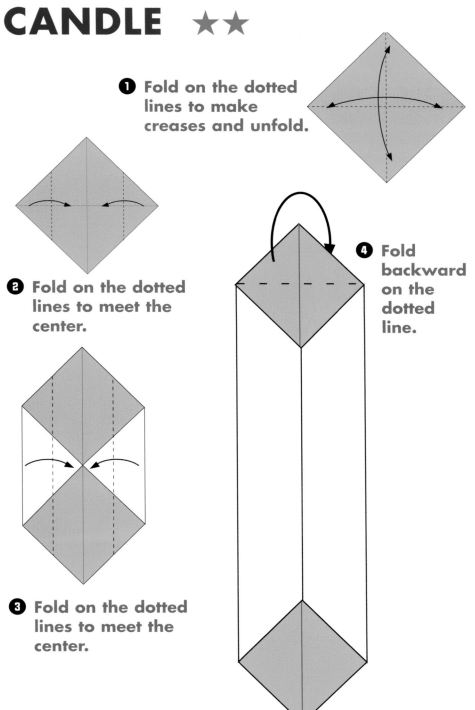

**❺ Fold on the dotted lines.**

**❻ Fold forward on the dotted lines.**

**❼ Step fold forward.**

**❽ Open the pocket from ⌂ and flatten.**

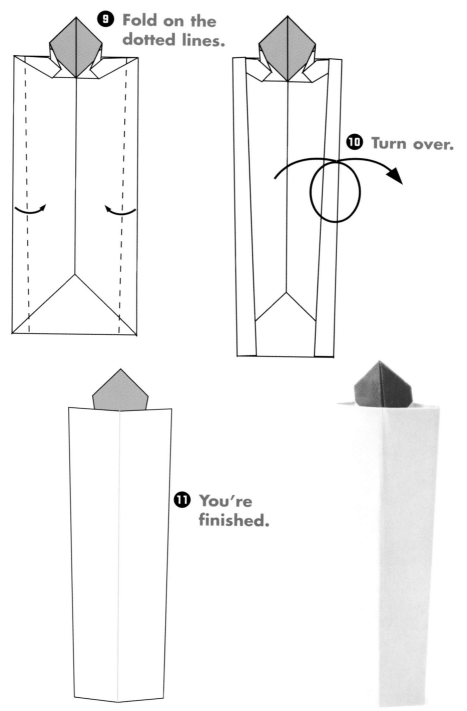

**9** Fold on the dotted lines.

**10** Turn over.

**11** You're finished.

13

# CHRISTMAS TREE ★★

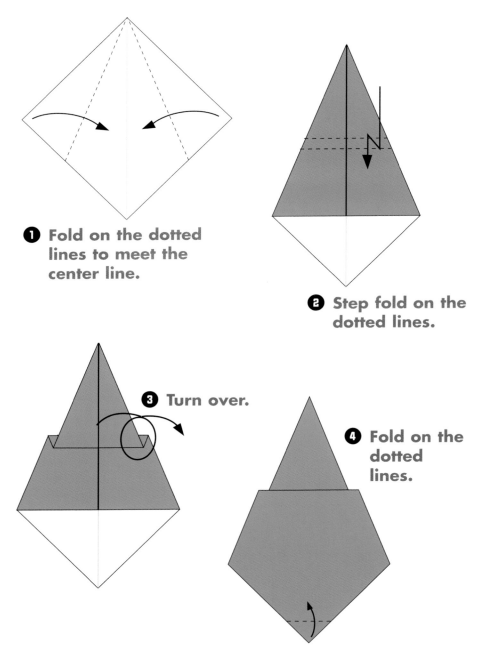

**1** Fold on the dotted lines to meet the center line.

**2** Step fold on the dotted lines.

**3** Turn over.

**4** Fold on the dotted lines.

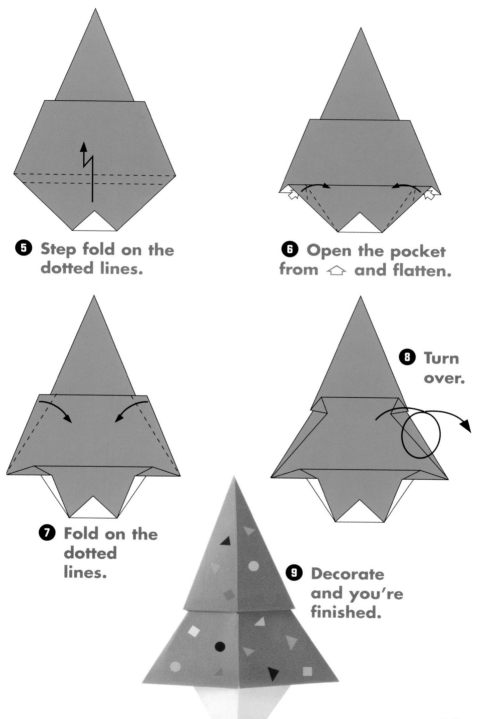

**5** Step fold on the dotted lines.

**6** Open the pocket from ⬆ and flatten.

**7** Fold on the dotted lines.

**8** Turn over.

**9** Decorate and you're finished.

15

# SANTA ★★★

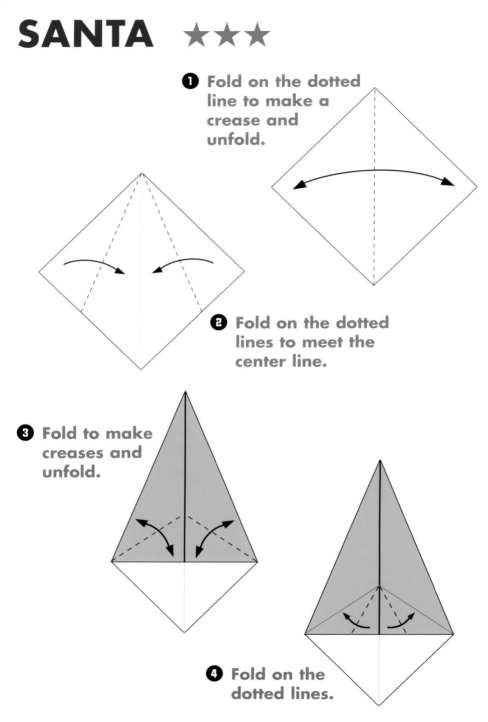

**1** Fold on the dotted line to make a crease and unfold.

**2** Fold on the dotted lines to meet the center line.

**3** Fold to make creases and unfold.

**4** Fold on the dotted lines.

**5** Fold on the dotted lines.

**6** Step fold on the dotted lines.

**7** Step fold on the dotted lines.

**8** Turn over.

**9** Fold on the dotted line.

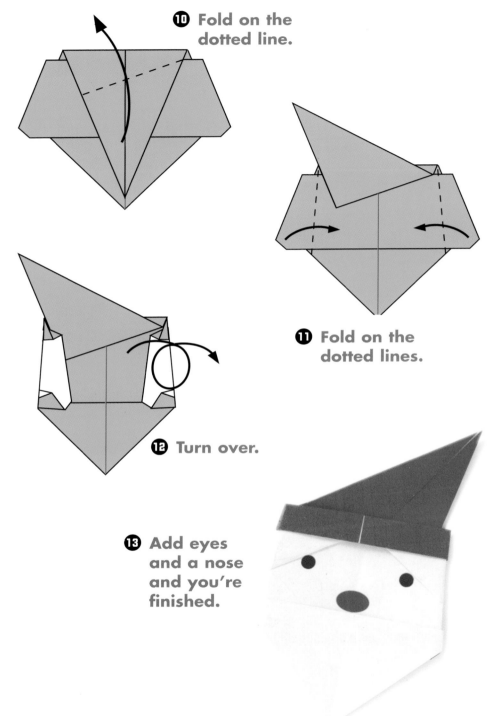

**10** Fold on the dotted line.

**11** Fold on the dotted lines.

**12** Turn over.

**13** Add eyes and a nose and you're finished.

# SNOWMAN ★★

**❶ Fold in half.**

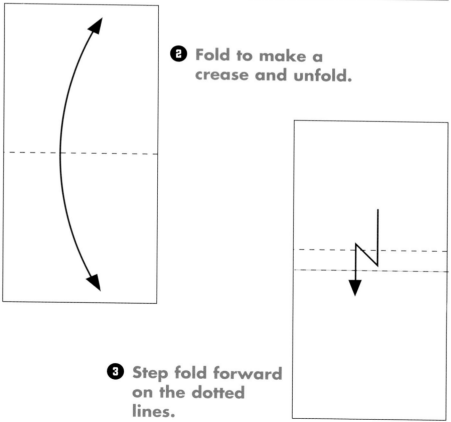

**❷ Fold to make a crease and unfold.**

**❸ Step fold forward on the dotted lines.**

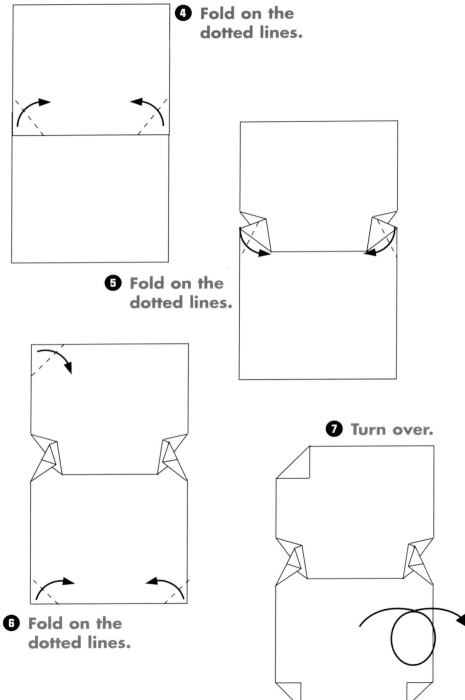

**4** Fold on the dotted lines.

**5** Fold on the dotted lines.

**6** Fold on the dotted lines.

**7** Turn over.

20

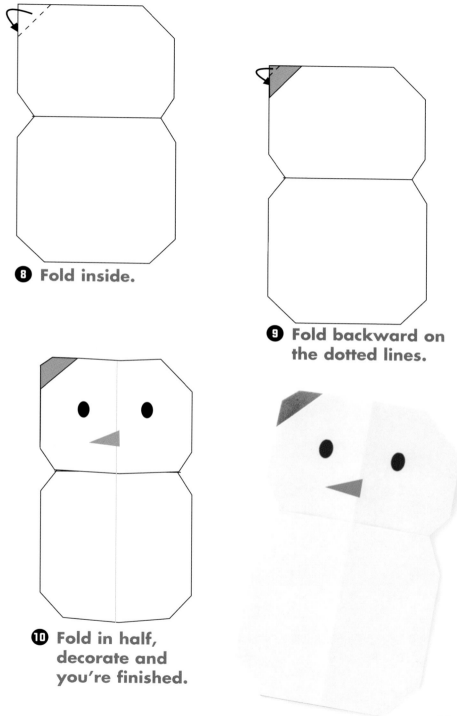

**8** Fold inside.

**9** Fold backward on the dotted lines.

**10** Fold in half, decorate and you're finished.

# BELL ★★★

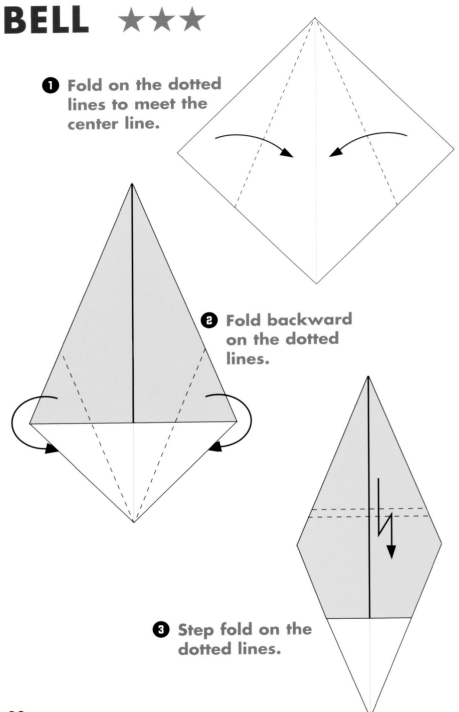

**❶** Fold on the dotted lines to meet the center line.

**❷** Fold backward on the dotted lines.

**❸** Step fold on the dotted lines.

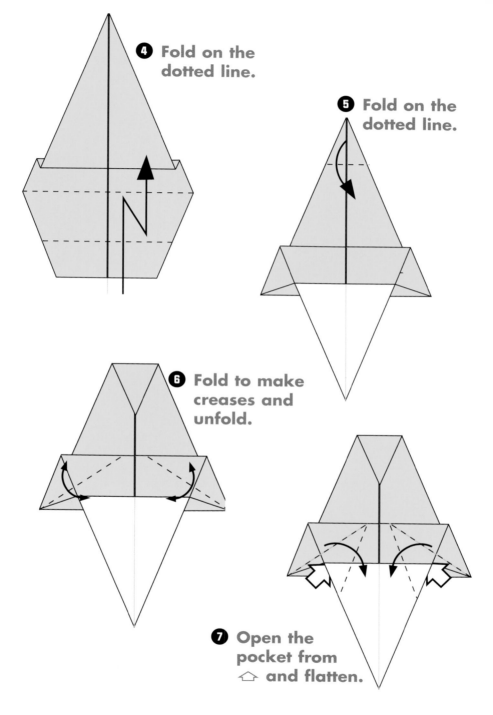

**4** Fold on the dotted line.

**5** Fold on the dotted line.

**6** Fold to make creases and unfold.

**7** Open the pocket from ⬦ and flatten.

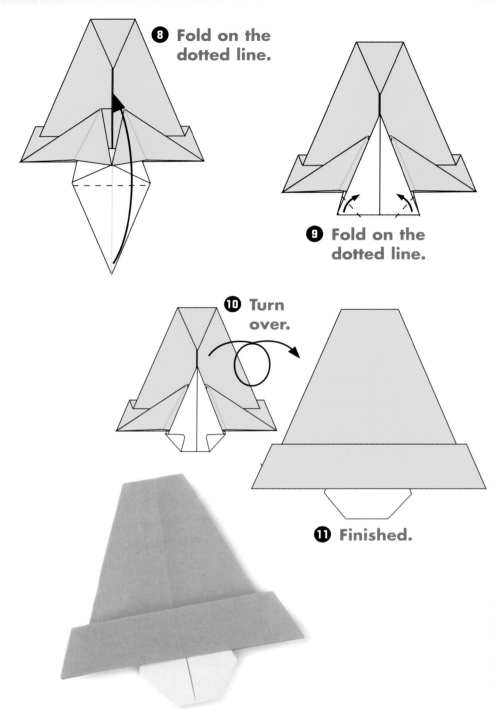

**8** Fold on the dotted line.

**9** Fold on the dotted line.

**10** Turn over.

**11** Finished.

24

# HANUKKAH

# DREIDEL ★★

1. Fold on the dotted lines to make creases and unfold.

2. Fold on the dotted lines to meet the center line.

3. Fold in half.

4. Fold on the dotted line.

$\frac{1}{2}$

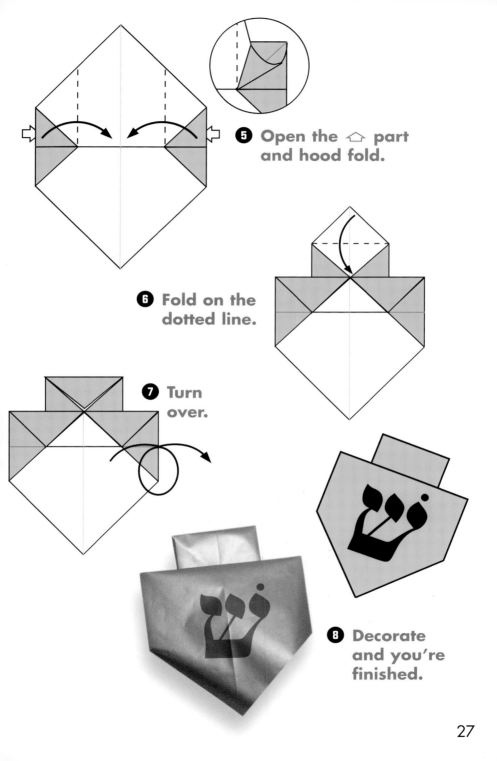

**5** Open the ⌂ part and hood fold.

**6** Fold on the dotted line.

**7** Turn over.

**8** Decorate and you're finished.

# THUMPING HEART ★★

**❶ Fold on the dotted lines to make creases and unfold.**

**❷ Fold on the dotted lines to meet the center line.**

**❸ Turn over.**

**4** Fold on the dotted line.

**5** Fold on the dotted line.

**6** Fold on the dotted line.

**7** Fold on the dotted line.

**8** Fold and fold back.

**9** Turn over.

**10** You're finished.

Pinch both sides to make the heart throb.

# PRESENT ★★★

## BOX:

**1** Fold in half to make creases and unfold.

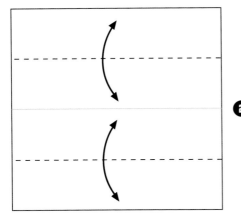

**2** Fold on the dotted lines to make creases and unfold.

**3** Fold on the dotted lines.

**4** **Unfold.**

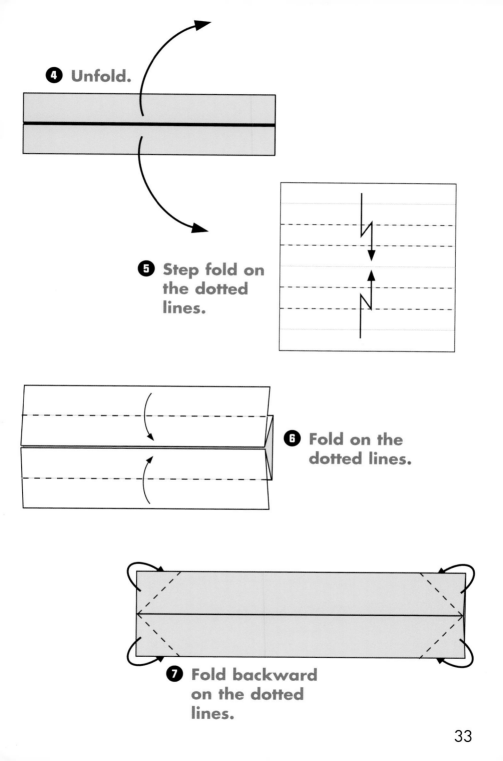

**5** **Step fold on the dotted lines.**

**6** **Fold on the dotted lines.**

**7** **Fold backward on the dotted lines.**

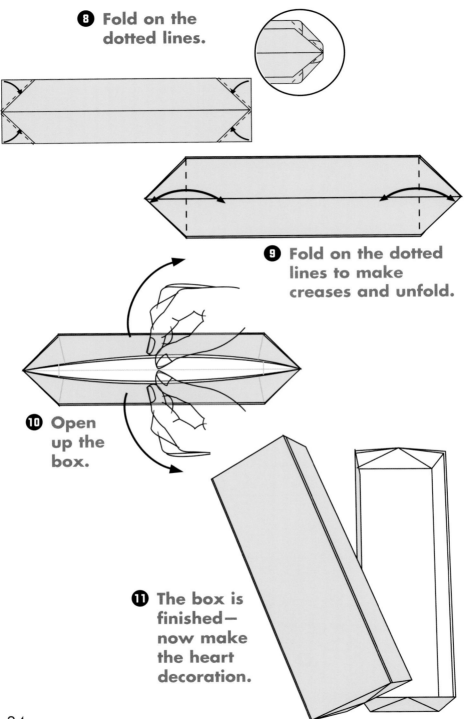

**8** Fold on the dotted lines.

**9** Fold on the dotted lines to make creases and unfold.

**10** Open up the box.

**11** The box is finished—now make the heart decoration.

# HEART DECORATION:
## (FOLD FROM ¼-SIZE PAPER)

**❶** Fold on the dotted lines to make creases and unfold.

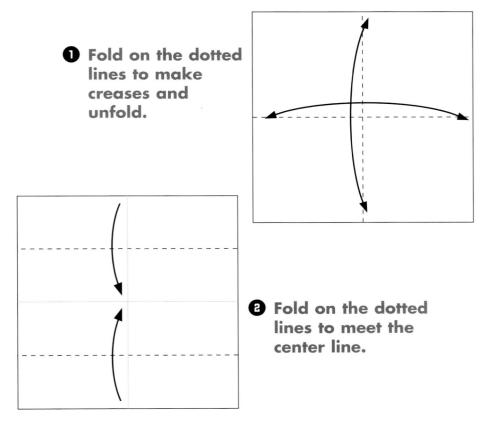

**❷** Fold on the dotted lines to meet the center line.

**❸** Turn over.

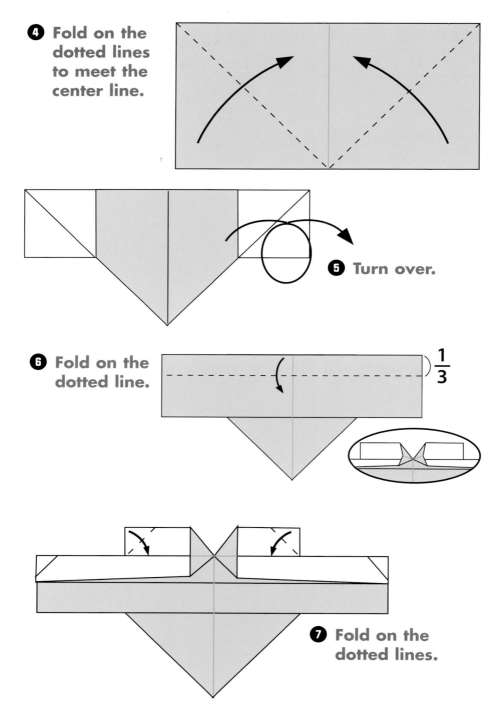

**4** Fold on the dotted lines to meet the center line.

**5** Turn over.

**6** Fold on the dotted line. $\frac{1}{3}$

**7** Fold on the dotted lines.

**8** Turn over.

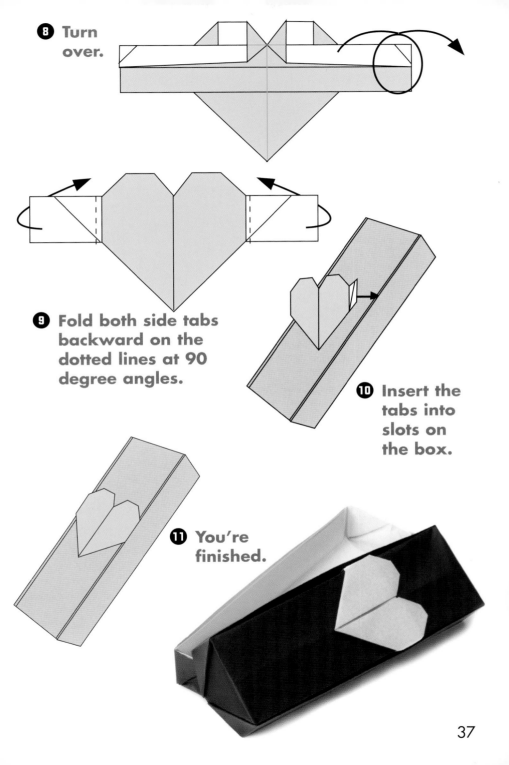

**9** Fold both side tabs backward on the dotted lines at 90 degree angles.

**10** Insert the tabs into slots on the box.

**11** You're finished.

# CANDY ★★★

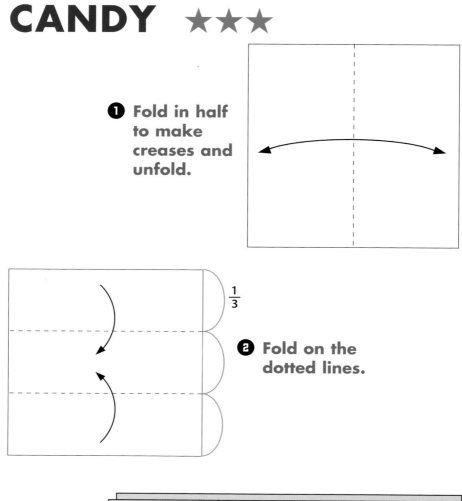

**❶** Fold in half
to make
creases and
unfold.

$\frac{1}{3}$

**❷** Fold on the
dotted lines.

**❸** Step fold on the
dotted lines.

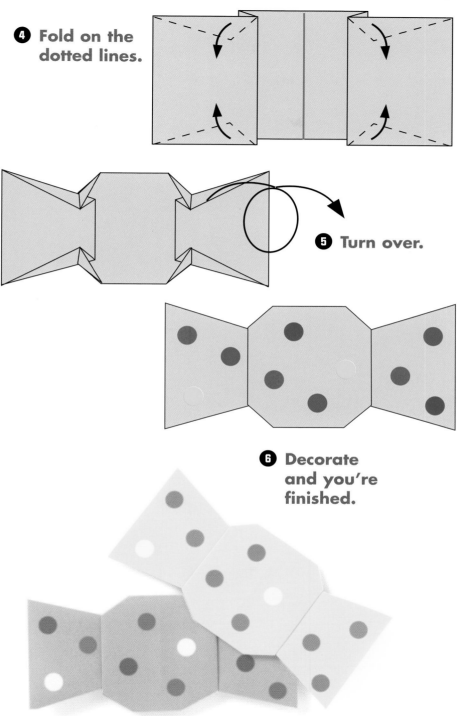

**④** Fold on the dotted lines.

**⑤** Turn over.

**⑥** Decorate and you're finished.

# EASTER BUNNY ★

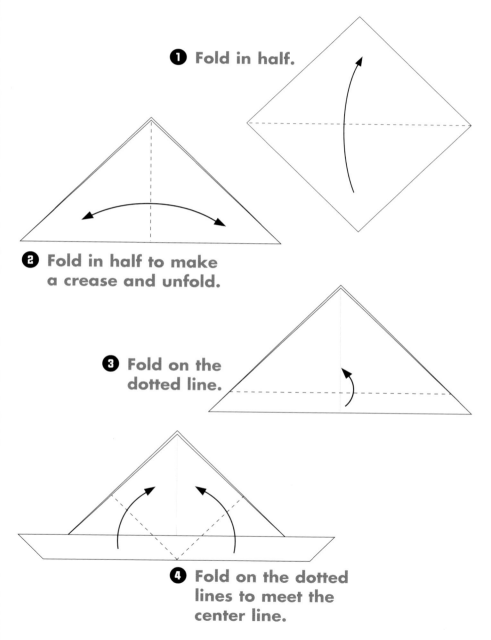

❶ Fold in half.

❷ Fold in half to make a crease and unfold.

❸ Fold on the dotted line.

❹ Fold on the dotted lines to meet the center line.

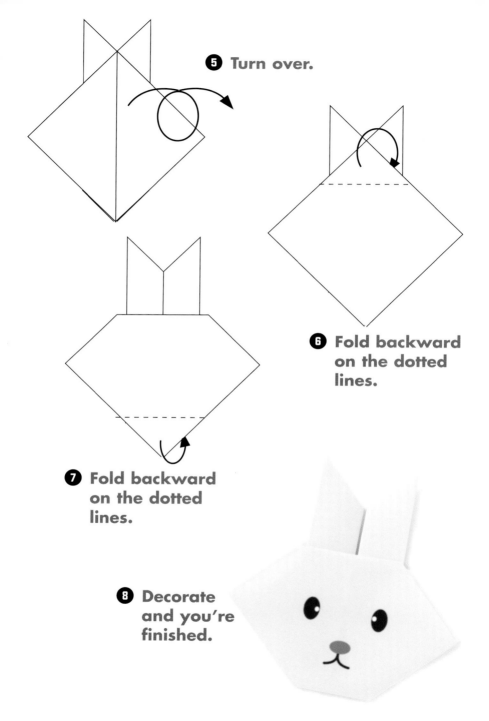

**⑤ Turn over.**

**⑥ Fold backward on the dotted lines.**

**⑦ Fold backward on the dotted lines.**

**⑧ Decorate and you're finished.**

42

# FLOWER ★★

## LEAVES:

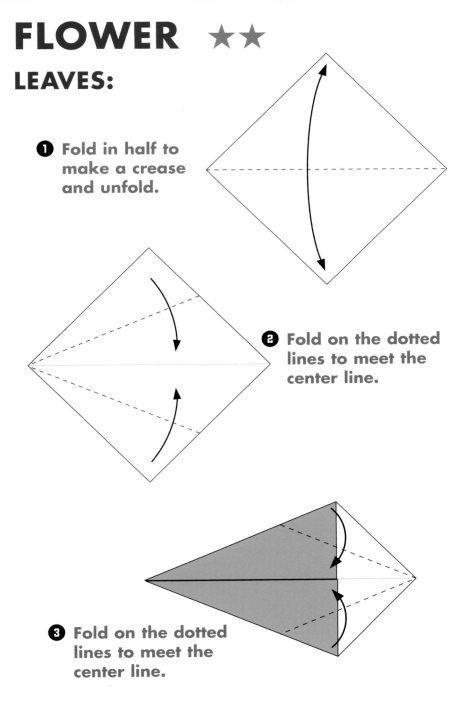

**1** Fold in half to make a crease and unfold.

**2** Fold on the dotted lines to meet the center line.

**3** Fold on the dotted lines to meet the center line.

43

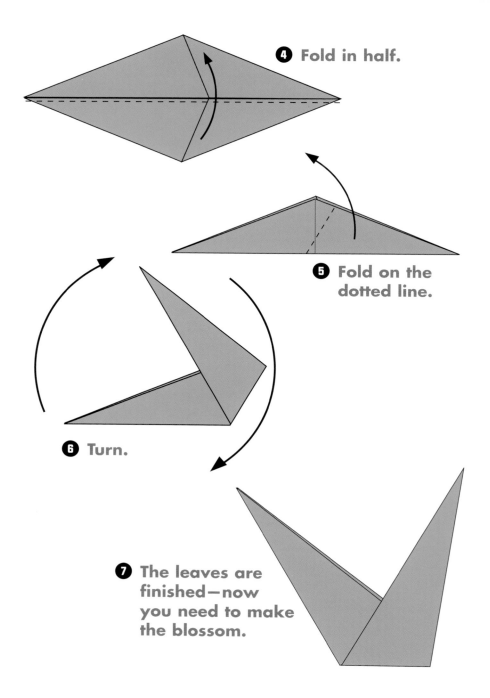

**4** Fold in half.

**5** Fold on the dotted line.

**6** Turn.

**7** The leaves are finished—now you need to make the blossom.

# BLOSSOM:

**❶** Fold in half to make a crease and unfold.

**❷** Fold on the dotted lines to meet the center line.

**❸** Fold on the dotted lines.

45

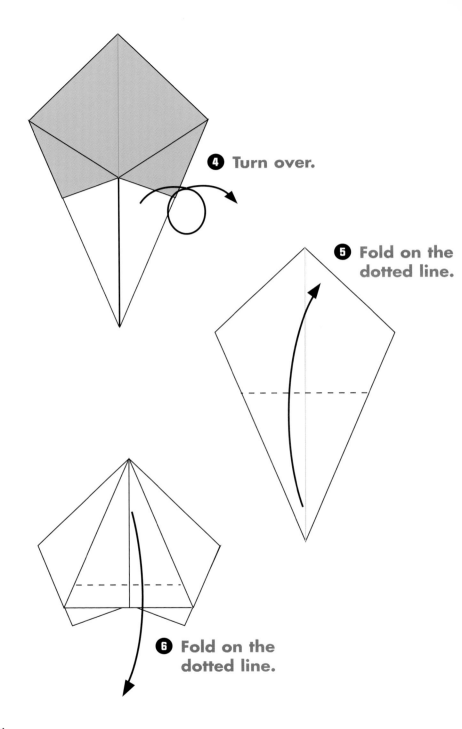

**❹ Turn over.**

**❺ Fold on the dotted line.**

**❻ Fold on the dotted line.**

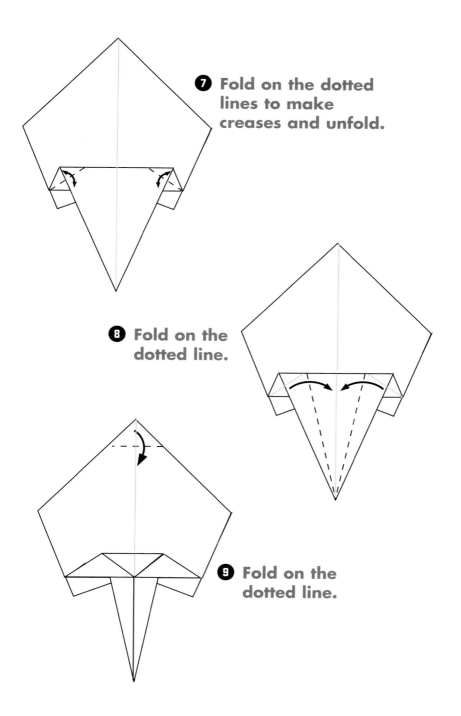

**❼ Fold on the dotted lines to make creases and unfold.**

**❽ Fold on the dotted line.**

**❾ Fold on the dotted line.**

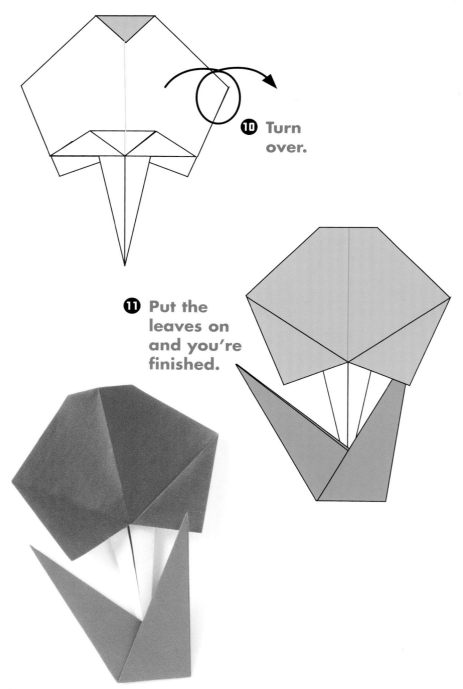

**10** Turn over.

**11** Put the leaves on and you're finished.

# HALLOWEEN

# BAT ★★★

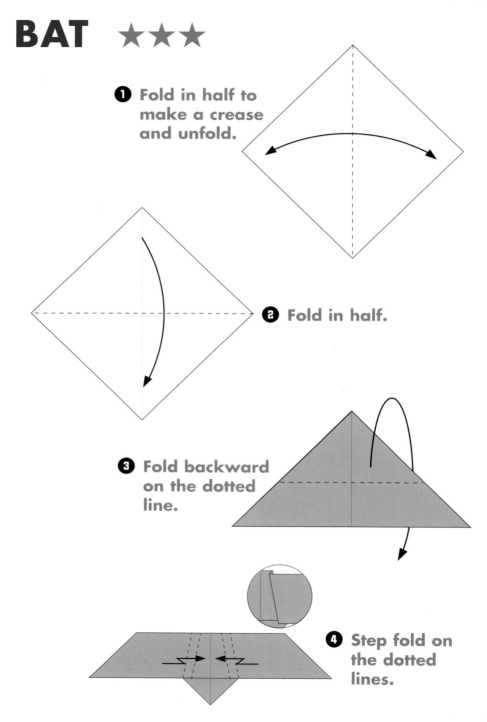

**❶** Fold in half to make a crease and unfold.

**❷** Fold in half.

**❸** Fold backward on the dotted line.

**❹** Step fold on the dotted lines.

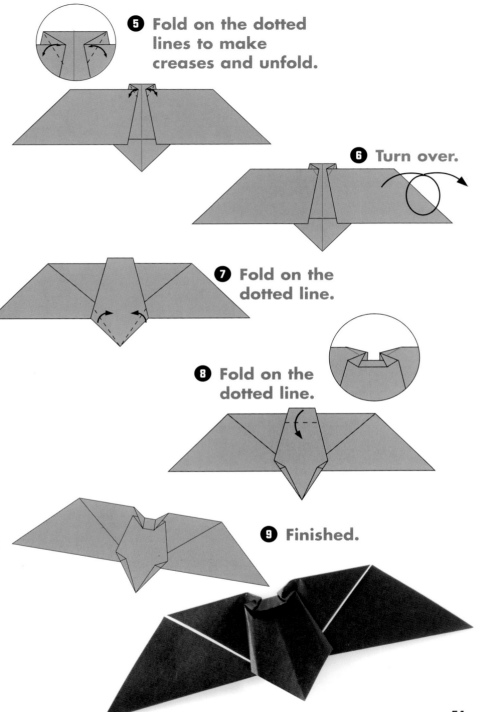

**5** Fold on the dotted lines to make creases and unfold.

**6** Turn over.

**7** Fold on the dotted line.

**8** Fold on the dotted line.

**9** Finished.

51

# GHOST ★★

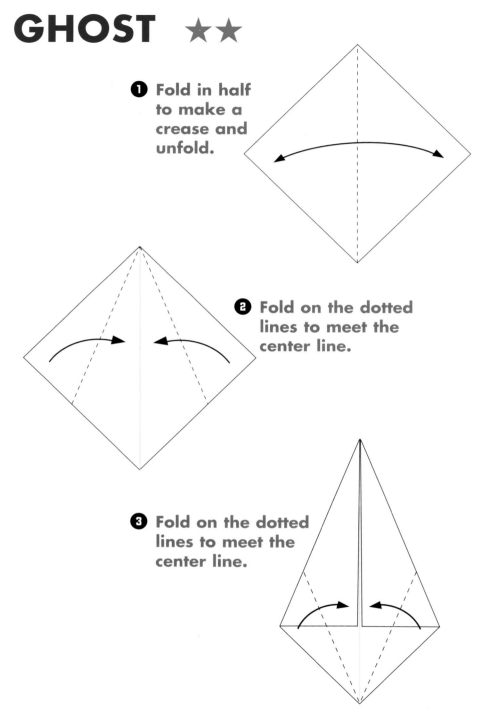

**1** Fold in half to make a crease and unfold.

**2** Fold on the dotted lines to meet the center line.

**3** Fold on the dotted lines to meet the center line.

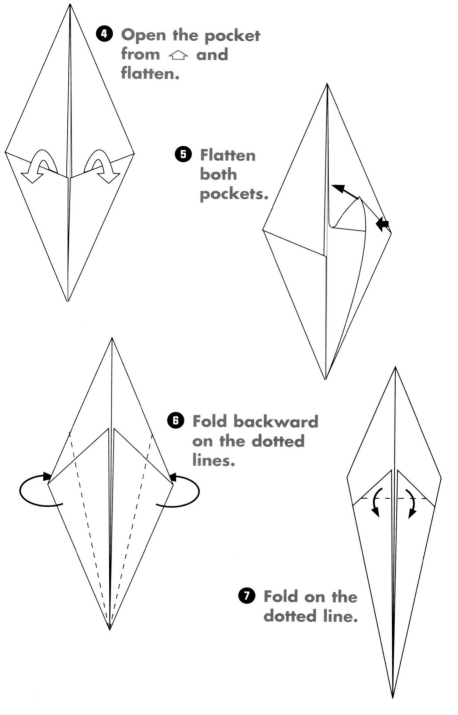

**4** Open the pocket from 🔺 and flatten.

**5** Flatten both pockets.

**6** Fold backward on the dotted lines.

**7** Fold on the dotted line.

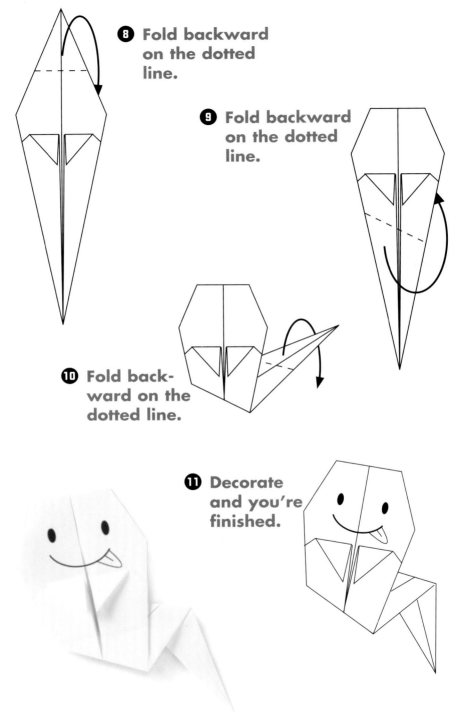

**8** Fold backward on the dotted line.

**9** Fold backward on the dotted line.

**10** Fold backward on the dotted line.

**11** Decorate and you're finished.

# JACK O LANTERN ★★★

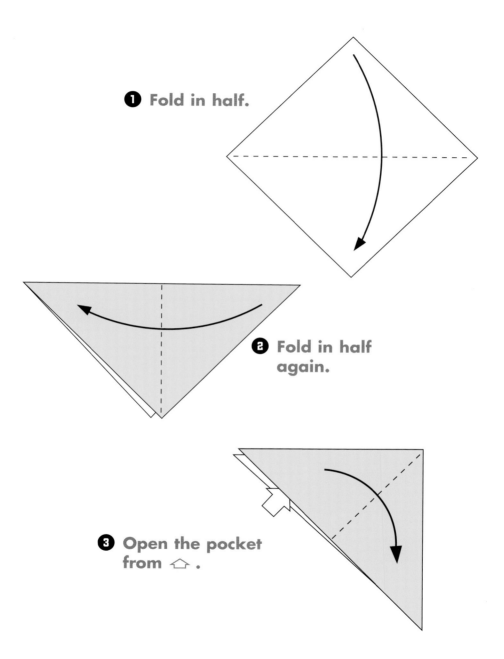

**❶ Fold in half.**

**❷ Fold in half again.**

**❸ Open the pocket from ⌂ .**

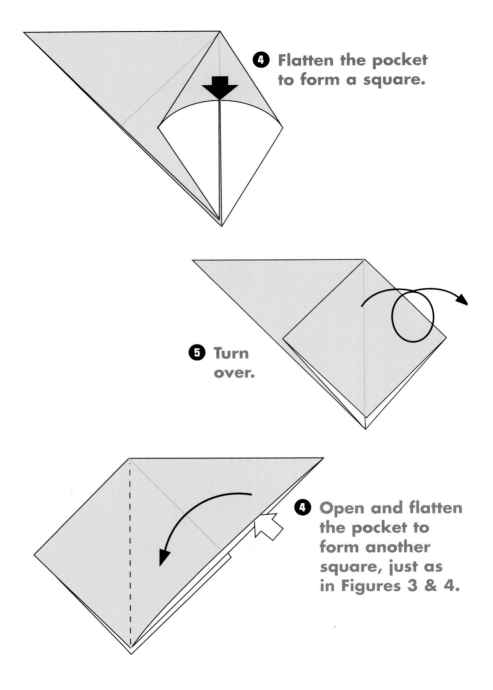

**4** Flatten the pocket to form a square.

**5** Turn over.

**4** Open and flatten the pocket to form another square, just as in Figures 3 & 4.

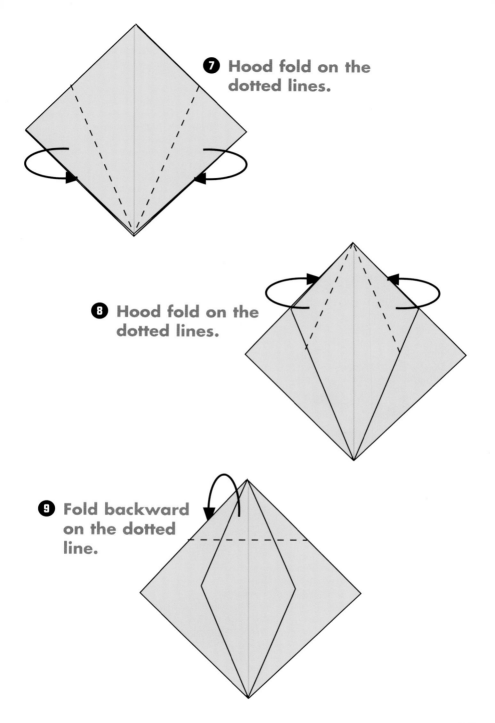

**7** Hood fold on the dotted lines.

**8** Hood fold on the dotted lines.

**9** Fold backward on the dotted line.

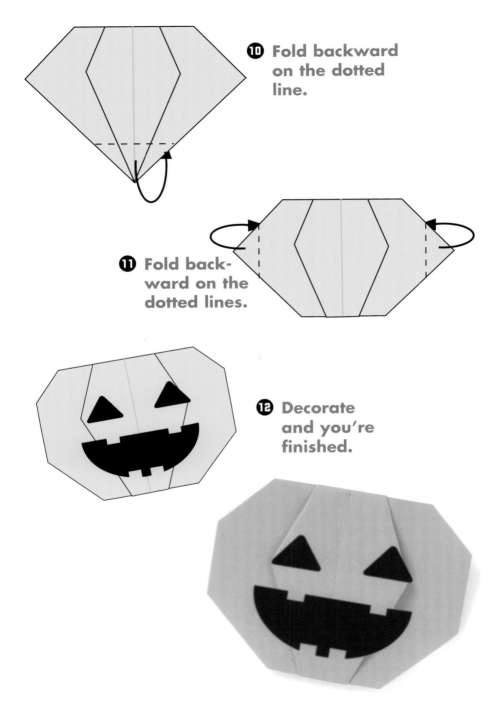

**10** Fold backward on the dotted line.

**11** Fold backward on the dotted lines.

**12** Decorate and you're finished.

# WITCH & BROOM ★★★

## BROOM:

**1** Fold on the dotted lines to make creases and unfold.

**2** Cut with a pair of scissors.

**3** Fold in half to make a crease and unfold.

**4** Fold on the dotted lines to make creases and unfold.

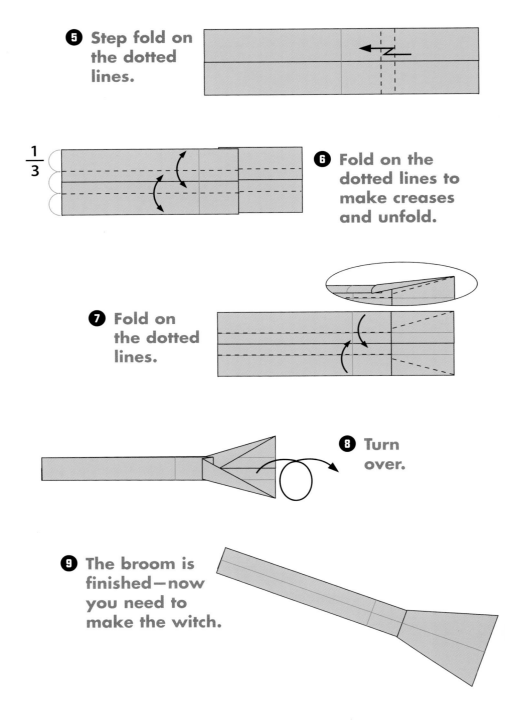

**5** Step fold on the dotted lines.

$\frac{1}{3}$

**6** Fold on the dotted lines to make creases and unfold.

**7** Fold on the dotted lines.

**8** Turn over.

**9** The broom is finished—now you need to make the witch.

# WITCH:

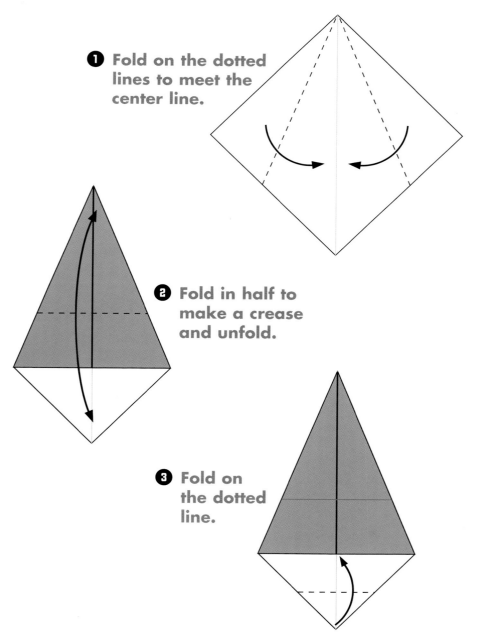

**1** Fold on the dotted lines to meet the center line.

**2** Fold in half to make a crease and unfold.

**3** Fold on the dotted line.

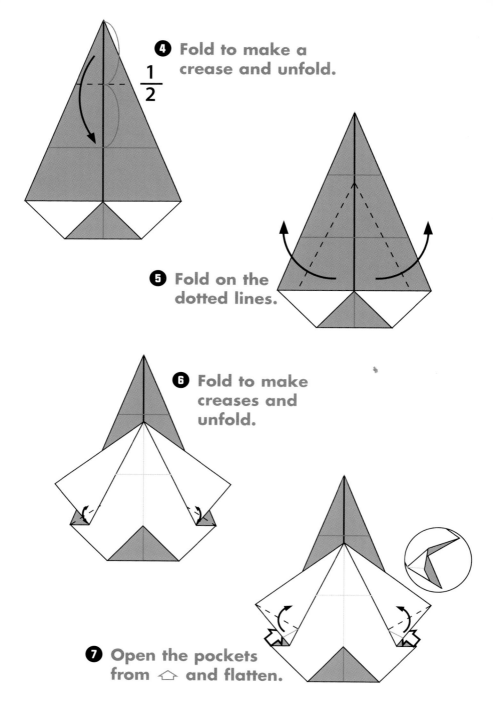

**4** Fold to make a crease and unfold.

$\frac{1}{2}$

**5** Fold on the dotted lines.

**6** Fold to make creases and unfold.

**7** Open the pockets from ⌂ and flatten.

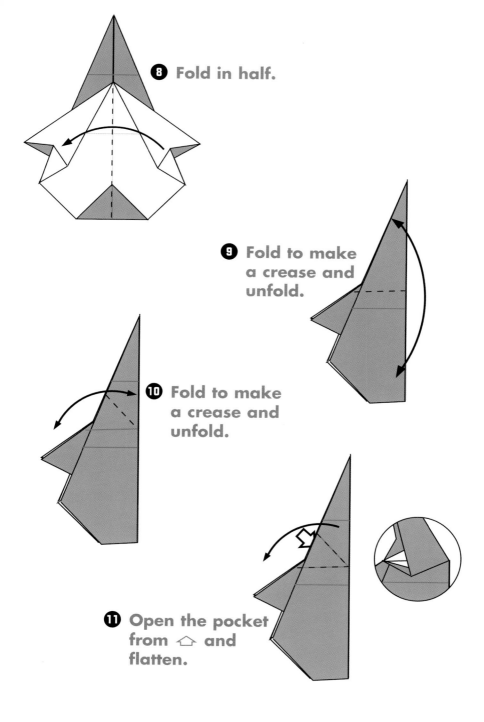

**8** Fold in half.

**9** Fold to make a crease and unfold.

**10** Fold to make a crease and unfold.

**11** Open the pocket from ⌂ and flatten.

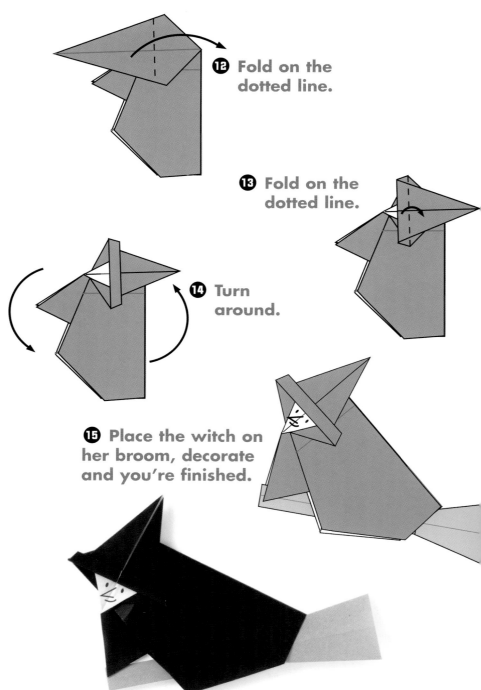

**12** Fold on the dotted line.

**13** Fold on the dotted line.

**14** Turn around.

**15** Place the witch on her broom, decorate and you're finished.